Scan Me! It's Fun

Preface

This book was originally created to be a journaling 'guide', designed to help you understand the best ways to mange, track and record your emotions while trading the financial markets. However, due to issues with the distribution of journals, the information needed to be separated from the original guide. As you read through *this* book titled 'The Emotional Trader,' you will often see references to 'My Emotional Trading Journal Guide.' This is the original version of the book which contained 3 months of journaling space, alongside the information you are about to read.

The information found in this book is designed to help you create a structured way of de-constructing your own emotions, and on chart behaviors. Trading Psychology is more than 80% of the battle when it comes to success in trading. So often I see traders do everything they can to learn a strategy, not realising that it is their own emotion which is the very thing that is holding them back from success. Whether the emotions are subtle or obvious, it seems not to matter, and takes a trader a long time to realise this the area that needs improvment. As you read through this book you will notice I often refer to three main areas of trading; Before, During, and After any trade. These are the areas which you will need to give your attention to in order to improve your overall trading.

While the journal itself is designed with many benefits to help improve your trading behaviors, the most important part is the reasoning behind each segment you are journaling. If you wish to purchase a *Hard Cover* Journal of the one mentioned in this book, designed to enhance this process, then please do so by scanning the QR codes at the beginning and end of this book. It will contain the keywords (you'll learn about this later) as well as six months of journaling space, monthly reviews, and the trading plan example.

However, if you choose not to purchase a journal, I highly encourage you to create something similar, that incorporates each section discussed within this book and is laid out in a similar way. The journal I refer to in this book is the exact journal I use daily to keep on top of my trading and is the number one reason I reached the level of trading I have. Doing this properly and consistently truly is life-changing. Please enjoy, but more importantly, please implement what you learn, and give it a few months of consistent effort. I guarantee you will see growth and development in your trading.

About the Author

Jake is a young Entrepreneur, 6-figure Trader, Trading Educator, Podcaster, Author, and a new Father, who, after years of struggling to find that discipline in trading, has now found the key concepts in each phase of his trading that enabled him to reach that highly sought-after accomplishment of 6 figure trader. He has worked tirelessly to get to the position he is in today and is now focused on helping others break that repeating cycle to create the success they are after.

Through intensive self-analysis of his journey as well as that of many of his students, Jake was able to decipher a few major similarities among struggling traders. However, the way these similarities presented themselves was not always so clear. Thus came the birth of 'My Emotional Trading Journal.'

Originally from the very isolated city of Perth, Western Australia, Jake left a comfortable Engineering job to pursue his passion for travel and exploration. At 25 he packed his bags, and left indefinitely, with the hopes to see all corners of the world, but what he found was worth a lot more than the travel pics. In the hunt for a way to earn while on the go, Jake was introduced to the world of trading and was hooked from the very beginning.

After almost 4 years since his first introduction to trading, Jake can happily say he has found the true freedom that he was originally seeking, it just so happens he found it in an unexpected place. Along his journey, he has faced many ups and downs, and seen a lot of his fellow traders fade away and give up on their pursuit and their dreams. Now he has shifted his focus to providing some of the clearest, step-by-step processes that he feels will help any trader regardless of their level or time on the charts.

Understanding yourself when you are on the charts, truly is the fastest way to achieving the success you desire. Trading is a 'you vs you' game, and it's only by understanding yourself to such a deep level that one is truly able to master their 'on-chart' behaviors and get on top of their trading psychology, and therefore the desirable account growth we are all after

.

My WHY?
(The Secret Motivator)

My Affirmations. READ ME, DAILY!!

(The Door)

Trading Objectives

HOW MUCH AM I WILLING TO RISK PER TRADE?

WHAT ARE MY GROWTH TARGETS?

> Daily:
>
> Weekly:
>
> Monthly:
>
> Yearly:

Defining the trader:
> What style of trader am I?
>
> What pair(s) do I trade?
>
> What time(s) do I trade?
>
> What days do I trade?

Knowing your strategy:
> What are my entries? Preferred entry?
>
> What are my exits? Failsafe exit?
>
> Where do I put my Stop Loss?
>
> Where are my Targets?

Trading Rules

Habits needing improvement

Good trading habits

Welcome

(Hello!)

Welcome to the next level of your trading journey. Your decision to purchase *this* particular journal shows that you are serious about developing your skills as a long-term, profitable trader; you are ready and willing to dive deeper into understanding the important role emotions play in the markets, and how they affect us as traders. This journal will help you understand and get on top of *your* emotions in trading, which is paramount to getting to that next level of trading success.

Have you ever wondered why so many people attempt to learn how to trade, but very few become successful in the long term? Perhaps you have been trading for a while and find yourself making the same mistakes over and over again. Have you ever said the words, "Why do I always do this?" Maybe you have traded well for a couple of weeks but have then blown it all in one fell swoop? I want you to ask yourself why you are yet to break the cycle. Why are you struggling to make those necessary changes? Why is it so hard to do the very things we know will improve our trading? How is it possible that traders with *all* the technical knowledge still aren't profitable?

Emotion. That's all it is, our inability to analyse, control and rationalise our emotions in unexpected circumstances. Very few people are capable of thinking emotionlessly and in probabilities. Does that mean very few people can become profitable traders? No, of course not. It just means you need to put the time into learning yourself at a very deep level, such that you know how and when *you* react to unforeseen circumstances in an unfavorable way. Then learn how to change or manage those behaviors.

My Emotional Trading Journal is *YOUR* Emotional Journal. It is designed to help you create daily routines, uncover your limiting beliefs, highlight some of your recurring bad habits, remind you of your good habits, and guide you through the constant tracking of both; your trades and your emotions. It will help your analysis and development, both on the charts and in the mind. Whether you have been in the game for a while and need to restructure, reinstate, or simply begin to define some rules and break through some barriers, or you are a new trader still trying to find your way in this seemingly simple, yet extraordinarily complex world of trading, this journal is for you. The idea here is for you to have a sort of companion that you use to help keep you focused on your objectives and guide you through the chaos that is…. *Emotion.*

As you work through this journal, please know that you will benefit most from taking your time, and completing each section with as much detail as possible. The first half of this journal is an explanatory guide that will walk you through the hows and whys of each different section. Don't aim to be perfect. It is intended that you and your *emotional journal* develop as you develop in your trading journey. Over time, you should start to notice some familiarity in your behaviors and therefore your values in relation to money, which you can change as you see fit. Allowing you to become that long-term, profitable trader you so desire. My goal is that you benefit greatly from this journal and, in turn, continue to use it throughout your career as a trader, constantly tracking, growing, and evaluating both yourself and your trading journey.

Now, you may have noticed a few questions on the previous pages. Don't worry, we will get to those. For now, I want you to understand the idea behind this journal. As you work through this journal, you will be guided to, through, or in such things as; setting up your environment, understanding and establishing trading objectives, and setting up a trading plan. We will discuss the importance of knowing your exits, explain how emotions affect most traders, and exactly how you can use *this* journal to get on top of those emotions. It is an inevitable fact that you will need to make personal changes throughout this journey, developing not only your skills but also replacing your limiting core beliefs with new beliefs that will serve you. You must understand that the person who brought you to the idea of trading and the person you are today, are different from the one you will need to become if you want to get to the level of trading you are striving for. Almost every trader I know has gone on a personal journey of self-growth that allowed them to become the profitable traders they are today. They have made significant changes and understood how to break free from some subconscious limiting beliefs they once had. These changes include, but are not limited to: the ability to self-assess, take losses (without emotional impact), and understand how/why these losses occur. With this in mind, I ask you to approach this stage of your trading career with an open mind and try to let go of any ego or stubborn habits you may have developed in the past. As you read each section of the journal, I suggest going to the associated pages and filling out the information relative to your style of trading. You will then be able to use this journal daily, both before and after your trading sessions, to read through your trading plan, and trading rules. You will also use it to self-evaluate and understand your own emotions, resulting in a more structured and consistent style of trading. As you continue to dive deeper into who you are on both a trading and a personal level, you should start to notice some profound and enlightening growth.

Now let's get into it.

Table of Contents

Introduction

(The Beginning)

"Smooth seas do not make skillful sailors."

- African Proverb

I am almost certain that somewhere along your trading journey thus far, you have heard at least one of the following; "95% of retail traders lose money", or perhaps, "The number one reason most retail traders fail is......Emotion!" Or even from those who are skeptics, "Day trading is just like gambling." Have you heard of any of these yet?? If not, I'm sure it won't be long. As traders, these aren't things we generally like to hear, but the truth is, to some extent, all of those statements are true. Becoming a professional trader is a task that involves the acceptance of risk and undiminished perseverance, two things the majority tend to fail at. But why? Why does something as simple as clicking a button with a 50/50 outcome become so difficult? It is an interesting observation that shows how having access to all the money one could ever want at the click of a button, soon becomes the very thing that stops that said person from obtaining it. Hmmm. Why do you think that is?

Furthermore, how *DO* we get on the right side of the statistics and go from becoming a 'lucky gambler' to a consistent and profitable trader? Well, there are a few things to consider, and it certainly isn't a "one size fits all" thing. However, there *ARE* three major areas that, if you are willing to spend time developing them, are sure to dramatically improve your chances of success. I once found myself in a discussion with someone who claimed that all profitable traders are psychopaths. An interesting hypothesis, but one I believed had some flaws. So, if your trading success does not rely on your psychopathic tendencies, what does it rely on?

As I mentioned earlier, there are three main areas that are guaranteed to improve your trading if you give them your focus. All three are rather simple concepts but are either completely ignored, not understood, or not even considered important aspects of trading. These are; Consistency, Risk-Management, and Emotions. Once you learn to manage these key areas of your trading, it's guaranteed that your results will improve. However, you *must* work on **ALL** three areas simultaneously, especially as they are closely entwined. You should *consistently* evaluate your *emotions*. You should *consistently* *manage your risk* and you should observe how your *emotions* affect how 'you' *Manage Risk*. You see, I view trading in three different phases, each representing one of these key areas in need of your attention.

> Phase 1: Before the Trade - *Consistency*
> This is when the **Strategy** is made
>
> Phase 2: During the Trade - *Risk Management*
> This is when the **Money** is made (Or lost)
>
> Phase 3: After the Trade - *Emotion*
> This is when the **Trader** is made (Or not)

What's to Follow?

There are several sections to this journal guide; the introduction, the three phases of trading, a section on optimizing our learning by setting up our environment, the journaling sections, an example trading journal, and a monthly review section. All of these should be used in conjunction with each other to create a less emotional, more robotic style of trading, and thus, an all-around better trader.

I have created the journal in this way to guide any new (or experienced) trader, from the 'gambler' who enjoys the concepts of trading to a developed, long-term, self-evaluating, consistent, and profitable trader. By going through each of the three phases in fine detail, I aim to help you better understand and develop each of the areas mentioned above. Throughout this journal, I will discuss the concepts and areas I have adjusted along my own trading journey.

These are the concepts and ideas that have had a profound impact on the consistency of my results, as well as the results of many other traders I have interacted with. If you *are* a profitable trader, then perhaps you have already implemented many of these concepts, but whether you are currently doing none, one, or all of these, I would still implore you to go through each section, as you may pick up the important piece you have been missing or even begin to see yourself in a new light. It is obvious to me that, by purchasing this journal, you are looking for a way to improve yourself, which is fantastic. So this is my first invitation to you to let go of some of that ego or bad habits I discussed earlier. Don't be the person who says, "Oh, I've already done this, so I'll just skip ahead." We are constantly in a state of change, and if we want to keep growing we should always be self-evaluating and looking for new improvements. I highly recommend going through each section with a new set of eyes. After all, the growth you have already made may be exactly what you needed to see 'old' information from a different perspective. Lastly, I recommend going over these concepts every six months to ensure your environment, setup, and trading plan are all up to date with your current skill and understanding of both the charts and your ever-growing self.

The Real Reason We Fail as Traders

I believe the most common cause of failure in trading is the inability to differentiate emotions from probability. The most important and yet difficult thing to understand is the very contradictory concept that; *while trading must have absolutely no form of emotion, with each trade being based purely on probability and having no correlation to any of the previous events, the entire market moves solely on the emotions and human behavior of those who are entering trades into the market at any given time*. This is quite a convoluted concept, I would recommend going over it a few times until you understand this on a deeper level. You see, we need to realize that the chart, as you see it at any given moment, will move in direct relation to the *emotions* of everybody collectively trading at that particular point in time. However, although the charts move on emotion, to beat them, we need to assess each individual trade as systematically and as **emotionlessly** as possible. The ability to disengage emotion from your trade, relative to a set of predefined rules, is, in my opinion, the defining separator between the profitable trader and the more common *emotional* trader.

If you want to understand more of the psychology of trading and other ways to sculpt how you should think when investing, I highly recommend reading books such as; 'Trading in the Zone' by Mark Douglas, 'Trading Beyond the Matrix' by Van K Tharp, or 'Market Wizards' by Jack. D Schwager. The concepts shared in these books are extremely important and valuable for your growth as a trader, but well beyond the scope of this journal.

Before we begin, you must understand that almost all long-term profitable traders go through their process for trading like it's a subconscious routine, a habit, implementing **EVERY** step of their trading plan without conscious thought. You need to have your trading plan become so regular that it is almost boring. Not to say you shouldn't enjoy what you do, but, the ability to follow a defined set of rules without being instantaneously manipulated by the chemical changes that induce emotion, is going to become the critical aspect in preventing you from taking those account crippling large losses. Again, I want to remind you that losing is a part of trading. Of course, we would like to radically reduce the number of losses we take, nonetheless, we can not completely eradicate them from our trading, and believing you can, will most likely result in the inability to progress forward on your trading journey.

Your First Setup

To finish this chapter, I want to move you on to your first activity. I truly believe this particular activity is one of the most crucial aspects of chasing any goal or dream. It's the one thing that will keep you going when times get tough, and when you feel like giving up. Believe me, there will be times when you feel like giving up. Doing and *understanding* this one thing will help guide you on the right path as you chase whatever it is you are aiming for, whether it is business, trading, or even running a marathon. That is…..establishing your 'WHY'.

You *MUST*, I repeat *MUST*, know why you are here trying to become a trader if you want to get through the hard days. Are you here to get rich, really fast? (Sorry, probably not going to happen.) Are you here to find a way to work from home? Are you here because you want to travel and work from anywhere in the world? Perhaps you are here to win time. After all, this is a job you can do in as little as an hour a day. Maybe you are here for the personal development that comes with becoming a successful trader. Perhaps you like the challenge, have something to prove or want to carve the way to a life of freedom for others to follow. Whatever it is, you need to define this for yourself. Truly knowing your why will become the driving force behind your success. It will be the first thing that you see every time you open this journal to come to trade, and hopefully something you will revisit on the days you aren't trading. The idea is that you are constantly reminded of exactly why you started this journey and can revisit it any time you may have had a bad day on the charts.

Step 1: Finding your 'WHY'

It is time to write down, with extraordinary detail, the exact reason you started this journey in the first place. I want you to turn to the very first page, and in the top third, write down your why. Why do you want to become a successful trader, and what will you do once you have "made it" as a trader? Do you want to buy that car, house, watch, or purse? Do you want to save the whales or build an orphanage? Perhaps you just want to quit your job. Whatever it is, write it down.

If you aren't sure of your exact 'why,' then I suggest researching an exercise called "7 Levels Deep." I first heard about this exercise from Dean Graziosi, and it is incredible for getting to know your true 'why.' If you would like some live, worked examples of this exercise, check out Episodes 22 through 26 of my podcast, "The Success Shift with Jake Snedker" which you can find on most streaming platforms, including Spotify, or by scanning the QR code found throughout this journal.

Step 2: Creating your Vision Board

Now I want you to go and find some pictures of your dreams/goals. I want you to spend time thinking about and physically getting images of your biggest dreams and desires and gluing them in, underneath where you wrote your 'why.' Go online and print them off, Canva.com can be great for this, as well as Pexels.com or perhaps, draw them if you can. You can put several things down here, but you must have a visual representation of what it is. You have now created your trading vision board. There are many reasons why doing this will set you off on the right path to success. If you want more information on why that is or are still having trouble figuring out your true WHY? You can check out my mini mindset course where I go through all these steps in detail and more, coming soon. For now, I want you to put this book down, and start brainstorming and completing Steps 1 and 2. Once you have completed those, then we can move on to Phase 1.

Phase 1

(Before the Trade- Consistency)

"Success is nothing more than a few simple disciplines, practiced every day; while failure is simply a few errors in judgment, repeated every day. It is the accumulative weight of our disciplines and our judgments that leads us to either fortune or failure."

- Jim Rohn

This quote by Jim Rohn helps to describe the difference between a newbie trader, and someone who has been profitable over a long period of time. Have you ever come across a trader who has been at this for years, knows all the technical analysis, but still isn't profitable? Maybe you are that person, and you just can't seem to understand why you still aren't seeing the results you so desire. Well, don't worry. If you can follow the steps given to you in this journal and CONTINUE to use them DAILY, you will soon discover why you haven't made it to that next level of success. There have been studies done showing that up to 98% of people fail when asked to do the simple task of writing down what they are going to do for that day, and then writing down what they did during that day, for three months, in exchange for a financial reward.

In a somewhat ironic sense, we as humans, through poor judgment and possibly boredom, find it immensely arduous to complete the simple tasks, day in and day out, that are required to accomplish the difficult task of becoming financially free through successfully trading the markets. If you can, for the next six months, do the following two tasks every day, without fail, I am certain you will see an improvement in your trading:

1) Fill out, 'Your Emotional Trading Journal' after every trading day/session.
2) Follow your trading plan/rules, without ANY deviation.

It truly is that simple.

To do these two things, you must first; get this Journal. Done! Congratulations, You're halfway there. (Physical copy is best). Second, make sure you have a solid 'Trading Plan' and set of 'Trading Rules.' If you need help with building/improving your trading plan, then feel free to head over to my 'Ultimate Trading Plan Course.' You can find it by scanning the QR codes. Remember, Phase 1 relates to everything happening before you enter a trade. It is about consistency and is where your 'strategy' is developed. During this phase, we need to get ourselves in the right frame of mind, reminding ourselves of our trading plan and our trading objectives, and guess what? We need to do this EVERY SINGLE DAY. This process should become a subconscious/automatic habit that you do naturally. To make accomplishing the aforementioned easier, I will break this phase into three sections. Affirmations, Trading Objectives, and Trading Plan, in that order. Note: your trading plan will span both Phase 1 and Phase 2, but we will get to that later.

Affirmations

First is our affirmations. If you turn to page two of this Journal you will see a page with the title, 'My Affirmations'. This space is for you to write a list of whatever you feel will help center you and bring you into the right frame of mind for trading. Now if you don't like the term affirmations, feel free to cross it out and header it with whatever you like. Maybe, 'Golden Rules of Trading', it doesn't matter. The idea here is simple. You need to spend at least five minutes before every session reading through this list to; A) Fill yourself with positive energy and bring yourself into that happy flow state, and B) Bring you from the outside environment, into the trading environment. After you have read the page, you can use the physical turning of this page as a metaphorical door that shuts out all emotional baggage from the previous days, including any emotion you may still have regarding previous trades. This is a door you can pass through, only once all previous emotions have been dropped (another reason to have a physical copy) and on days you can not do this, simply close the entire journal and step away from the charts for the day. You must leave all emotions, worries, and pretty much all other human characteristics at this door. It is time to switch on the systematic, mechanical or even robotic version of you, that is ready to do nothing other than follow your pre-defined rules.

Trading Objectives

On the very next page, you will see the title 'Trading Objectives' followed by a list of questions. I want you to get a *pen* and write down your answer to the first question in extra big font. Don't keep reading. Do it now!

OK, good. Did you write your answer in the form of a dollar ($) amount?? I hope not. If you didn't write your answer in terms of a percentage (%) then you seriously need to stop here and go learn about risk management and the beautiful power of compound interest. We will touch on this in Phase 2 but it is extremely important you already have a basic understanding of your risk. If you would like to learn more about this in-depth, feel free to get in contact with me directly. Information is in the back. If you *did* put your answer in percentage (%), I now want you to go over it again and highlight it. This risk amount should be so ingrained into you as a trader that it becomes something you don't ever have to think about. Now you can fill out the rest of the trading objectives. You should read through these every day after you have read your affirmations. Again, it should become habitual. The point of these trading objectives is to define the type of trader you are. You need to understand what works for you, as well as what your intention is for the day/session ahead.

On the next page, there is a section titled "Trading Rules" here you need to create your own personal rules designed for; A) Restricting any bad habits you may have. Use this to remind yourself of these bad habits that you have found regarding your trading, so you can avoid them during each session. A powerful tip when writing these rules is the way you phrase them. Don't be limiting and disengaging with your rules. Rather, see a different perspective and write them with a sense of positivity and misdirection. Example 1; "Don't overtrade." Could be, "Allow yourself to take only the VERY BEST trades. 2-3 is more than enough." Example 2: "Don't overleverage." Could be " Ensure you are practicing proper risk management." The difference in our language can create a different emotional attachment to the phrasing. Learning to trade can be hard. Rather than saying "I don't know how to do this," try "I haven't learned how to do this yet." See the difference. We want to start our day in a positive, friendly, and light manner, and rephrasing our self-talk is a simple but powerful way of doing this. B) Reinforcing any good habits that you may have developed so far. Energy flows where attention goes. Again we are aiming to start our day with a positive mindset, we want to be focusing on our good behaviors as much, if not more, than our bad behaviors. C) Recognising what your ideal trade setups look like. It is extremely important that you are waiting for the markets to come to you. If you know what your looking for you will find it easier to practice patience, waiting for only the best setups. I have left plenty of space for you to write these in as much detail as you possibly can. I suggest having only a couple of setups and restricting yourself to entering only these few trades. I have four. You can find an example of one of mine at the end of this chapter.

You may have noticed that directly under your risk, are your growth targets. These are also extremely important to understand. You must get into the habit of aiming for a certain growth (in %) per session. You are not here to win (X) number of trades or make (X) number of dollars. You need to stick to your rules and simply aim for a modest target of daily growth. It is at this point I should remind you that the estimated annual, yes annual, average growth for the S&P 500 is around 8%. I meet many traders who start off targeting +8% *per day*. Now, while this is possible, it is *very* unnecessary and will require either more risk or more time on the charts to achieve these targets consistently. I have completed an example below to show how an average daily increase of even 2% (when compounded) will significantly improve your financial future.

Compound Interest Calculations

$$Acc\ Bal.\ =\ Start\ Bal.\ \times\ (1\ +\ \frac{\%\ Growth}{100})^{No.\ of\ Days\ Compounded}$$

Example:

Starting Balance = $10,000

Daily Growth = 2%

Days traded = 250 (this is roughly one year of trading days)

$$Acc\ Bal. \ = \ 10,000 \ \times \ (1 \ + \ \frac{2}{100})^{250}$$

$$Acc\ Bal. \ = \ 10,000 \ \times \ (1.02)^{250}$$

$$Acc\ Bal. \ = \ \$1,412,677$$

Have some fun, change some numbers around and let your mind be blown by how quickly compound interest can change your life. I want you to play with this calculation and realize the power of what you have in front of you. Once you have finally wrapped your head around how mind-blowing these numbers are, I want to remind you of the importance of staying modest with your expectations. Rome wasn't built in a day, and neither will your fortune be. The key here is; _consistent action over time._ So I guess the next question you may ask yourself is: How do I get to that level of consistency? The answer: A solid 'Trading Plan,' and the discipline to follow it.

When I first learned to trade, I found that almost 90% of the discussion was based on finding a good trade. How do we find good trades? The perfect strategy, or so I thought. I spent so much of my time bouncing around from strategy to strategy, looking for that perfect 'edge'. I would find a strategy, have a few wins, and sometimes make a little bit of money, but then, when it didn't make me extremely rich within a few short months, I would simply move on to the next strategy. Which, low and behold, also didn't make me rich. Sound familiar? It wasn't until a few years in that I realized how much more there was to becoming a profitable trader. I came to understand that it wasn't the strategies that were faulty, it was my attitude and mindset that wasn't working properly. So I chose a strategy with an 'edge' that I thought suited my style of trading and I _stuck with it._ What is an edge you ask? An edge is simply that 'thing' that you have, that puts you above other traders. This could be a multitude of technical analysis techniques, price action, fundamental analysis, or a combination of the two. Technically it's your strategy, and it's what you use to determine whether or not it's a good time to buy or sell the market. So, whilst having a good edge, and knowing that edge very well _is_ extremely important, it is the one thing I will _not_ be discussing throughout this Journal. Instead, I will be focusing on the habits, behaviors, and development of emotions needed in trading, to get you to that _next_ level. At this point in your journey, you should already have settled on your strategy and know your edge very well. You are going to need this to set up your trading plan. If you haven't found your edge and are interested in learning the strategies I use and trading live with me and my team, then you can reach out to me personally via the QR code.

Trading Plan

There are hundreds, if not thousands, of trading strategies that will work to be profitable in the market. Some more than others. Some require more patience, some require more discipline and some require more time on the charts. However, *all* of them require a human ability to follow the trading rules exactly as they are laid out for the trader to become profitable with that trading style. Once there are deviations from the rules, then the trader is technically creating a new strategy. One which might not be proven to even work.

By creating a checklist of trading rules, you will soon find out where your focus needs to be, in order to progress further toward being that profitable long-term trader. Either through; finding a new strategy more in-tune with your trading preferences and personality, or optimally through improved personal development, and emotional intelligence.

There are many different ways to create a trading plan, and you need to understand what will work best for you. For this reason, I have tried to make this section somewhat general. I have also left an example of one of my trading plans at the back of this journal. Feel free to use this as a basis as you build your own, or if you like, you can use it as a direct template, swapping out the information to suit your strategy. Regardless of how your trading plan looks, you must print it out and keep it somewhere visible at all times while trading. If you would like an e-version of this trading plan, please get in contact.

As you can see in my trading plan, I prefer a numbering system. I find it easier to work with and believe it to be a simpler way of determining what the charts 'might' do. Remember, nothing is guaranteed when trading. When a trade I like, is setting up, I review my checklist and score it against my trading plan criteria. I use this score to decide the probability of the setup performing in the way I predict. Based on my scoring system, if it scores a seven or above, I will take the trade. If it scores below seven, I will simply not enter and wait for the next opportunity. The higher the score, the more probable it is, that the trade will go in my preferred direction. Don't be fooled. This system isn't a guarantor, it's just a guide. You *will* have a 10/10 trade that goes against you. This is the nature of trading. This system just reduces the probability and frequency that this will occur. Once I have scored my entry I review my exit checklist and determine the one or two exits I will use for my trade management. I always have two exits that I keep in mind when managing my trade. One is to minimize losses, should my trade not perform as expected, the other is aimed at maximizing gains. Sometimes as the chart progresses, your exits may change, however, this is not common, and it is good practice to avoid changing your exit strategy during a trade, as it is more often done when losing rather than winning. More on this in Phase 2.

Please note: There are many ways to set up a trading plan. You could use an, 'if - then' style, multiple choice, or even one set of HARD rules. Find out what works best for you. For me, it was the numbering system, and this is what I have used in this example. Again, I want to emphasise the importance of a detailed and descriptive trading plan. I would highly recommend checking out my 'Ultimate Trading Plan Course,' in which I break down in great detail all the aspects of a powerful trading plan, and explain why each section is important and how/when/why you should adjust and restructure your trading plan.

My Setup

The way I set up my checklist is to first think about my absolute ideal trade. For me, it involves a particular kind of price action candle, a particular position on the Traders Dynamic Index (TDI), and a trending chart. I also know that I am biased and favorable to buys. I don't know why this is, but I do know this about myself. It is important to be conscious of these things and consider them when searching for your setups, as they will often affect your 'NON-judgmental,' probability-based analysis of the charts. In a more technical version, my preferred trade setup is as follows;

A Bullish Engulfing candle, after my fast-moving average on the TDI, crosses the middle line of my Bollinger bands, whilst the 50 EMA cuts through the price action candles immediately after the red and yellow (5 and 13) EMA's have shifted, *and* with no previous structure in the way to act as resistance.

As you can see, this is a fairly specific set of circumstances, and that is why it scores a perfect 10/10 trade for my style. I then use this as my base marker for my point structure. I take my 'edge' and break it down into a subset of points that increase as my trade tends to be closer to my ideal trade setup. I use the particular areas of my strategy to separate and denote different levels of points. As you can see in the example trading plan on page 178, I have a section for price action, and one for the TDI. Perhaps you use 'Fibonacci' as part of your strategy and could denote different points for each fib level you use. Maybe you use 'Harmonics' and could adjust your points on the percent ratio of each move. Or perhaps you use 'Point of Control' and can base your points on varying volumes. Whatever you decide, it needs to be specific and defined for you.

After this, I go through the combination of points assigned and aim to find a minimum value for which I can associate a high enough probability for a profitable outcome. As you can see in my example, my minimum trade score is seven. You may not have as many variables as I do, or you may have many more. So choose your numbering system carefully and apply it as you see fit. Your checklist can also be improved through time spent back-testing. As you can see, these trading plans will vary drastically depending on your strategy. Nonetheless, the key points are....

1) Figure out what your perfect trade looks like
2) Separate your different trading methods
3) Break them down into varying strengths
4) Establish a score that has a high enough probability for you to risk your capital
5) Order this checklist so you can quickly and easily review it for EVERY trade. Ensuring you are taking only THE BEST chart setups, EVERY! SINGLE! TIME!

This checklist is designed to stop you from adjusting your strategy due to the ambiguity of different chart environments. Spend the time doing this properly once, and you will save yourself a lot of time and confusion in the future.

Now that you have your checklist and have it structured in a way that benefits you, it is time to find your optimal trades. Great! It works. You are finding the same great trades, over and over again, based on your ideal trade setup. But STOP. We aren't even close to finishing. Once you have found your setup and are interested in buying/selling, we then move on to Phase 2. The first half of this trading plan/checklist is exactly what we will use, to consistently find the same trade, time and time again. Although, this is not enough for us to be profitable. Before entering our trade, we must establish our risk and our trade management system. Remember, Phase 2 is where the money is made. We must incorporate these aspects into our trading plan and add them to our mechanical trading rules.

Phase 2

(During the Trade - Risk Management)

"Risk management means protecting oneself from the adverse and unexpected decisions others may make and, in the process, making better decisions than they do."

- Peter Bernstein

"My mission isn't to make money in bull markets. My mission is to preserve capital."

- Michael Price

The unfortunate truth about day trading is; the majority of people who it appeals to are those who, by their very nature, enjoy taking risks. Unfortunately, this 'ability' is a double-edged sword. When learning to trade, it is imperative that you, as a trader, can establish the probability of your desired outcome *as well as* the risk for *every single* trade you make. The issue arises when we become complacent, accepting risk without quantifying it. All too often, I see traders start this journey because they like taking risks and living differently from the 'norm.' Perhaps, living life on the edge, on their terms. Does this sound like you at all? Don't get me wrong, these are all good traits to have, and the ability to take risks **does** help us in trading. However, these characteristics also make following rules and sticking to a plan rather difficult. It is a little ironic how the very thing that brought us to the idea of trading is also one of the biggest reasons we struggle to progress. You see, without the ability to consistently quantify your risk and relate it to the probability of your desired outcome being correct; success in this field is somewhat unlikely. The process required for an individual to become a rule-abiding risk-taker can be extremely arduous, especially if you live by the philosophy; "rules are made to be broken." I know because this was my philosophy when I started. The changes you will undergo on this journey are like no other, and it's for this reason I refer to trading as; "the best personal development program in the world." Remember, the person you were when you started this journey, simply can *not* be the same person who will make it to the 6, 7, and 8-figure trading accounts that we all desire.

Hopefully, you now understand that this isn't just about taking risks but also managing our risks to account for any unexpected decisions made by the bigger players in the game. It is this ability to manage your risk properly, and protect your capital that allows your trading plan to be profitable over a long period of time. Continuously adjusting your trading plan due to the influence of your weekly or even daily performance is much like jumping from strategy to strategy. It doesn't allow you to gather a true understanding of the longevity and sustainability of your methods, and behaviors. The entire reason you have a trading plan and practice Risk-Management is for *long-term* profitability. I need you to understand that successful profitable traders are here for the long term. Remember, you are now in Phase 2. This is all about the time spent during the trade and is where all your money is made. The best way to enhance this is with proper Risk-Management and sticking to **YOUR** trading plan.

In Phase 1 you established a set of solid trading rules (or a Checklist) based on your trading style, that will allow you to consistently find trades with a high probability of success. Great, but does this mean you are ready to enter the trade? Not yet. Before entering *any* trades, you first need to establish and quantify your risk. This means; becoming *completely* prepared to lose any or even all money you are risking within this specific trade. You must know exactly how much you are willing to relinquish, in the 'hopes' that the trade will perform in the way you are expecting. Please understand that nothing is guaranteed in trading and you must always be prepared for every outcome possible. Protecting your capital to the best of your ability.

Establishing Risk

How do we properly manage risk? Well, by now you should have completely transitioned to looking at your accounts and trades in terms of percentages rather than dollars and points. To begin, I would suggest finding a certain amount of money that you would be content with simply giving away and just starting there. You will know that you are risking too much if you are feeling stressed or anxious when you are in drawdown at this amount. As your experience grows, so too can your risk. Thus it is always best to start low. Please don't forget; **YOU SHOULD ONLY BE INVESTING MONEY THAT YOU ARE COMFORTABLE LOSING.** Now, this will be different for everyone, depending on your relationship with money and where you are in life, and your trading journey. For now, I would suggest starting with a fairly generous but standard value of 2%. Whatever you decide on, it should be written in your trading objectives, at the very top of the second page of this trading journal.

To correctly quantify our risk, we need to understand the relationship between the percentage of the account we risk, and its dollar value. As everything on the charts is valued in points, pips, or pipettes, I have provided you with the following equation. The key to correctly and consistently calculating our risk is understanding lot sizing. This is your broker's link between your account value in dollars and the number of points made per trade. The calculation is as follows.

$$\text{Lot Size} = \frac{(Risk\% \times Account\ Size)}{(100 \times Points\ in\ SL \times Contract\ Size)}$$

Say I have a $20k account and want to risk 2% per trade. To figure out what lot size I should use, I first need to find where I will be placing my 'Stop Loss,' and thus the number of points (or pips depending on your instrument) I am willing to risk.

That's right, a 'Stop Loss.' I am sure you have heard of it before. You should be using one on every single trade you make. Without fail. If you choose not to, that is your choice, however, I would see this as very poor risk management. With that said, trading is an individual thing and you must stick to your style of trading. If you do *not* use a stop loss, then please utilize Phase 3 of this trading journal guide.

For this example, I will use a stop loss of 50 points. Remember, I am a scalp trader on US30. I also know that my particular broker allows a contract size of 10 for this instrument. So my lot size calculation will look like this......

$$\text{Lot Size} = \frac{(2 \times 20{,}000)}{(100 \times 50 \times 10)} = 0.8$$

To remain within my risk tolerance for this trade I would need to enter a trade with a lot size no bigger than 0.8 lots. Now we have established our risk. The second half of Phase 2 looks at trade management. Just as we did in Phase 1 for the trade set-ups, we must now do, in Phase 2 for our 'Exits.' Having a process for exiting a trade is just as important, if not more, than your plan for finding a trade.

Trade Management

Unfortunately, the majority of traders are much more comfortable holding onto a losing trade in the hopes that it will turn around rather than holding onto a winning trade allowing for maximum gains. To reduce this issue and eventually reverse this phenomenon, we must create a set of predefined, mechanical rules to help with our exits. Again these rules are going to vary depending on your strategy. For some traders, your exit plan may consist of many options according to various situations and indicators. For some, these rules may be very simple. Nonetheless, it is important to have them written down and visible so that each of your trades gets managed in the same manner. For example, your strategy may be as simple as setting a 'Take Profit' and letting the trade do its thing. In this case, rules are needed, regarding where to set the 'Take Profit.' Is it at a set distance in points? Is it 2x your stop loss away? Is it set below/above the previous structure? These aspects of your trading plan need to stay consistent for you to be a long-term, profitable trader.

Other trade management rules could include details on; When to move your stop loss to break even? Do you trail your stop loss in profit? Do you take partial profits at particular levels? Do you move stop loss due to price action events? Do you have exits relative to EMA's or the TDI? You can look at the example trading plan in the back for ideas, but be sure to spend time understanding your strategy and implementing rules relative to you. It is OK to have a few very simple rules, as long as they are followed *every single time*. One important thing to mention here that I touched on earlier is the common issue of changing your exit strategy during your trade. You will notice in Phase 3, that you're asked to write your exit plan before you take your trade. Many traders will allow emotion to take control during their trades and create a justification of why changing their exit strategy is a good idea. Let me assure you, it is **not**. In very *very* rare occasions it may be beneficial, but don't let this be the slippery slope that leads you back to inconsistent trading. I mentioned earlier that I tend to have two exits in mind - one for minimizing losses, and another for maximizing gains. I still declare this to be the best practice. Creating your 'Exits' checklist should complete your trading plan.

The First Half Recap

Now it's time to recap. So far we have established the reason you began trading, your 'why,' and created a vision board. We have outlined your trading objectives, goals, and some affirmations (or trading rules) that you should be living by, while on the charts. We also created a set of mechanical trading rules/trading plan that will help you establish your ideal trade relative to your strategy, *with consistency*. Lastly, we have developed an understanding of proper risk management and constructed a system for managing that risk and maximising our profits. The ideas outlined in Phases 1 and 2 should help with your consistency, risk management, and trade management. Combined, you will develop a stronger strategy that allows for consistent high-probability trades, and the ability to maximise profits, without being emotionally sucked into the individual trade. The concepts discussed in Phases 1 and 2 are critical foundations that any successful trader will need to become profitable. However, the real key to *this* journal is in Phase 3. What most people don't teach, and what few traders manage to conquer, is themselves. Phase 3 is about what happens after the trades have been made. Phase 3 is *all* about emotional analysis and where all of the personal expansion happens. It is here, that you will discover your subconscious values and beliefs. It is here, that you will make quantum leaps. It is here, that you will find what truly requires improvement.

What good is it having the perfect strategy if we can not follow it? Why implement risk management if our emotions are always adjusting it? What's the point in exits if our greed takes over and causes us to stay in the trades? Why trail our stop loss if our fear manipulates it every single time? Having a good foundation is extremely helpful, but what good is it if we are unable to understand ourselves? What good is it if we are unable to understand *why* we do what we do, in the moment, and *why* we behave the way we do when real money is on the line? If you are going to pay attention to one section of this guide, make it Phase 3, as this is where **TRUE** growth happens.

Phase 3

(After the Trade - Emotions)

"If you can learn to creat a state of mind that is not affected by the market's behavior, the struggle will cease to exist."

- Mark Douglas

There is no denying the many benefits associated with tracking your trades. But what is even more beneficial than tracking your trades? Tracking your emotions, throughout each trade. As I mentioned earlier, there are hundreds, if not thousands of trading strategies that are proven to work. I am hoping, by this stage in your trading journey, depending on where you have learned to trade, that you are focused on one particular strategy with a proven track record. However, just because you are learning a strategy that has been proven to work, does not mean that you should be having success. Why? Because the variable withholding that strategy from producing significant financial gains is **YOU**. More directly, your emotions.

Fear and Greed

The entire global financial markets are run on emotions. Mainly *fear* and *greed*. At the fundamental level of economics, we have supply and demand. If people **FEEL** a particular, let's use the term 'asset,' will be of greater value to them in the future, the demand for it will increase, as will the price. If people are **SCARED** that the asset will lose value in the future, they tend to sell it, creating an increased supply and thus, a drop in price. Many factors will affect the feeling one has towards a particular asset. Regardless of the reasons, action is taken once there is a sufficient build-up of emotion, and depending on which emotion and how much someone has of it, determines how drastically they will buy or sell. In fact, the 'fear and greed index' was created for this exact reason. Aimed to help investors understand whether a particular asset is over or under 'hyped' and to prevent them from getting carried away with their emotions. Another useful tool for understanding fear and greed, if you haven't seen it already, is the wall street cheat sheet shown below. I suggest studying it thoroughly as it explains the psychology of emotion in any market cycle very well.

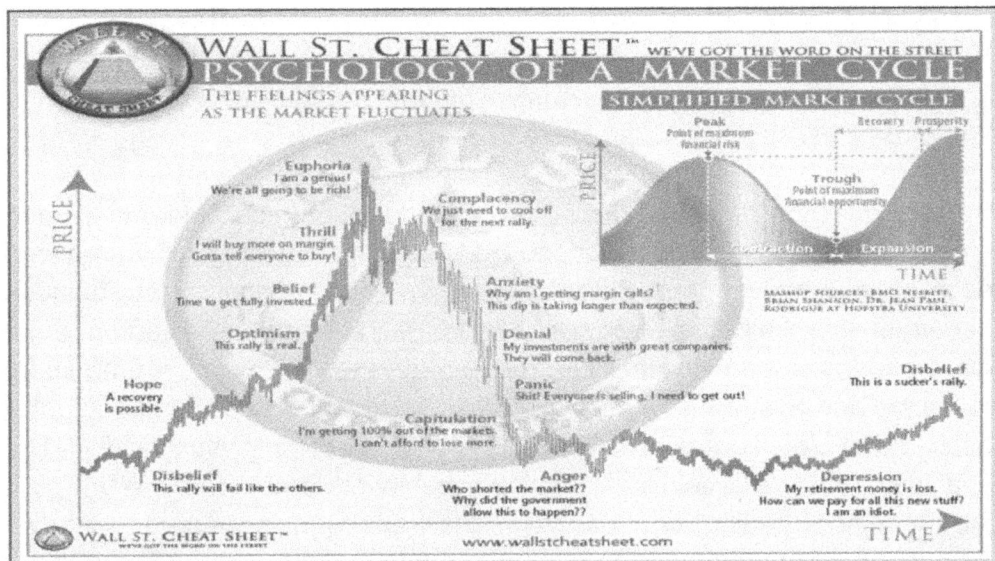

Hopefully, this gives you a better understanding of the importance emotion plays in trading. But how do we use this information to our advantage? Well, if the majority of traders fail due to emotions, then we need to track and understand how we respond emotionally to what happens on the charts. In turn, we can train ourselves to think in probability and eradicate emotions from influencing our trading decisions, allowing us to stick to our trading plan without letting our fear or greed manipulate our actions. With this, we can buy the fear and sell the greed, the opposite of what the majority of traders are currently doing.

The Discovery

For months I was told to; track my trades, create my plan, and organize a checklist. As easy as these things were to do, they were just as easy not to do. I quickly fell into a comfortable rhythm of what I would call, 'So very close to successful trading.' I had a good edge, I was consistent, and I had a good understanding of technical analysis, however, I wasn't getting the account growth I desired. It wasn't until I went through the process of actually doing the things that were suggested to me, that I realized some of the bad personal habits I had. These included: Changing my choice of exits when in a trade, rather than using the one I had decided upon before entering the trade. Not exiting a trade that failed to do as I anticipated, and instead went sideways, thus changing the analysis needed to predict the market, relative to my strategy, without *bias* from my original entry. These are just a couple of the many things I noticed about myself. This does not necessarily mean they will be the changes you need to make. Nevertheless, until you start doing the things the professional traders do and following the rules meticulously, you will struggle to see that change and most likely struggle to get those desired results.

So the question remains: How did I figure out these bad habits and emotional drawbacks? You guessed it. Tracking. Tracking (or journalling) each of my trades, and more importantly, my emotions through these trades, is what helped me see who I was as a trader and as a person. Even more important than tracking the trades and emotions, was the time spent reflecting and analyzing what I had tracked. This reflective time, spent after each trade (or trading session) is key to becoming successful. The analysation of one's self and emotional behaviors and responses whilst in the moment of trading, *is* what makes the trader. It can even be as little as 20 minutes after each session but *must* be done, every time. This is Phase 3 and this is where the trader is made.

The How to…

There are many intentional design aspects to this journal. Below I will explain how to utilize these and why the journal has some of its particular features. Of course, how you use it is entirely up to you. I just feel that if you understand why it was built the way it was, you may be able to get maximum use out of it, thus accelerating your learning process and giving you the results you are chasing.

To start, this journal is designed to allow tracking of both the basic information from your trades and the emotions during each phase of the trade in one easy place. It has been designed for use with any strategy and any style of trader, from swing trading to scalping. Please know that I am predominantly a scalp trader and this is where the basis of the design comes from. Although, I do also swing trade cryptocurrency and have therefore made it functional for all styles.

The first thing you may notice is that the information for each trade spans across two pages, in one consecutive line, with only five lines on each page. This is to limit the number of trades you are taking during your time on the charts. Now I do understand some trading styles are based on the quantity of trades, not quality. For those strategies, unfortunately, I feel this journal may not be the best way for you to track your trades. Though for the majority of traders, especially as you progress to a more professional level, it becomes much more about waiting for the charts to come to you and only entering the *very best* trades that match your trading plan. Over-trading is a *very* common problem amongst most new traders. It is the idea that the more trades we enter, the more likely we are to catch those 'BIG MOVES" and come out with a positive outcome. The truth is, this is the opposite of what generally happens. Continually trying to catch those big moves without proper analysis (and risk management) is how you lose money. That is the definition of getting sucked into the fear and greed cycle that runs the markets. As explained earlier, to be profitable on the charts we need to do the things that most traders are not. Jumping into several trades in the hope that it will go our way, based on a feeling, is the surest way to become another loss statistic.

Most successful traders will tell you, "it only takes 1-2 *good* trades to reach your daily goals." If we trade with patience and allow the charts to come to us, we *really* shouldn't be taking any more than 3-4 trades in any given day/session/week depending on your style. It is for this reason I have limited the number of trackable trades on each page to five. My suggestion would be, that each page represents a day/session for scalpers, a day for intraday traders, and perhaps a week for swing traders. If to start, you are still overtrading, I suggest writing a big '2' on the next page with a highlighter to brightly and boldly signify that you are using two pages for tracking per day/week. We will use this as our first main visual cue for self-evaluation. Another suggestion, if it works for your style of trading, is to write the day of the week in the top corner of each page so you can later discover your most profitable trading days.

Page 1:

As we move through the journal from left to right, you will notice how we transition through the phases, recording our emotions as we go. Now, depending on your style of trading, you may need to wait until after the trade to fill in this information, but when possible, I would recommend doing it in the moment. If you need to go back, give yourself the time to fill each section honestly and ensure you go into detail. This will help get you the best results out of each section.

On the far left, we begin with basic trade information that will help you to gain knowledge on; the time, pairs, and types of trades that best suit you. The first column can be filled in as soon as the trade has been taken.

> **Date:** The date you entered the trade - For those who hold trades over multiple days, I have left room above to put the date you exited the trade.

> **Time:** The time you entered the trade - This will allow you to understand which sessions are best suited to your style of trading. For example, you may notice that all trades within 10 minutes of 'market open' end with a loss. After a few months of these observations, you can look to avoid this time.

> **Pair:** The instrument that you are trading - Tracking this may allow you to reduce some instruments that are less successful for you.

> **B/S:** Was your trade a Buy or a Sell? - Often, we will have a bias in one direction or the other, and sometimes our strategy works best in bullish markets compared to bearish and vice-versa.

The next four columns you can come back and fill in after the trade has been closed. These are placed together, so we can easily see all the basic trade information in one location.

> **W/L:** Was your trade a Win or a Loss? - If you 'broke even' you can place a '-' or simply leave it blank.

> **T.T:** This is your 'Time in the Trade' - It can be useful to record this. Sometimes we sit in trades too long, just moving sideways or we hold on too long, giving back some of the profits. Sometimes we are

too fearful and protect our trades too quickly. If you quantify an optimum length of time to stay in a trade, relative to you, then you can adjust to the style of trading that best suits you.

W.T/C.T: Are you trading With the Trend or Counter-Trend? - Counter-trend trading often needs a different style of management. If you notice you are not profitable when counter-trend trading, then maybe it is best to stick with the trend. Alternatively, you may find that you trade better going against the majority.

P/L: This is where you record your Profits or Losses - As mentioned earlier, you should now be seeing, both profits and losses, in the form of a percentage (%). This is, by far, the best way to create a good mindset capable of embracing the power of compound interest. In this box, you will record your % of profit/loss.

Now that we have our basic trade information in one spot, it is time to explain your reasoning behind the entry you decided to take. One very common reason many traders fail is due to the 'NO ENTRY ENTRY.'[1] This describes a trader who just hits the button for fun and can not justify the reasoning behind why they made this particular trade. This is one of my 'Performance Review Keywords' which I will elaborate on, later in this chapter.

Box 1:
Here you are asked to describe your entry in detail. This should involve all aspects of your edge, as well as *anything* you are even a little bit concerned about. More often than not there are many reasons to enter a trade. However, as you get more experienced it is often more helpful to look for reasons not to enter a trade. If you have a large range of knowledge, from different trading styles, be cautious. Crossing strategies can become quite debilitating and you may find yourself never entering a trade at all. This box is designed to help you find out what you are noticing on the charts and what you may be missing. This information can then later be used during backtesting to see where you could improve, so be sure to add as much information as possible.

---

[1] This is a term I first heard from my trading friends Leah Stark and Amy Vanderraad-Koutsopodiotis.

Box 2:

This box is our first box of emotions. Here, we want to write everything we were feeling just before we pushed that button. Did you feel rushed to enter? Were you unsure about your stop loss? Maybe you were only 50/50 on this trade before entering, which left you feeling a little anxious. Perhaps you were super calm and 100% confident in this trade. Great. Write this down as well. Any thoughts that ran through your head before entering should be put in here. These are the emotions we experience during Phase 1 before the trade is made.

Box 3:

The last box on this page is for our emotions during the trade. How did you feel as the trade played out? Were you stressed as it moved into drawdown? Did it turn and go the opposite way on you? Maybe you were hovering above the close button for fear of being wrong? Many things can happen during a trade, both expected and unexpected. This box is where you will record all of it. If you find you're an anxious trader, try grabbing your pen after entering the trade instead of hovering above the close button. Writing down your thoughts and emotions may be just the thing to distract your mind enough to allow logical thought back in.

Page 2:

As we move over to the second page on the right-hand side of the journal, you will again see a column of four boxes. These are aimed to track your exits and the overall feeling of your trades.

> **Exit Strat:** What was your desired exit strategy before entering the trade? - We shouldn't be entering trades hoping they go up or down. We should already have, in our minds; a take profit level, a rough risk to reward, and an idea of how we will respond if the trade does not go our way. Your strategy may be as simple as setting a 'Stop Loss' and a 'Take Profit,' that is ok. Write it down.

> **Actual Exit:** What was the reason this trade closed? - Did it hit your 'Stop Loss' or 'Take profit'? Did you trail your 'Stop Loss'? Did you manually close the trade because an exit appeared? Did you close the trade because you were happy with your profits? It is important to know why you exited a trade. During backtesting, you may find that you can adjust your style to allow the trades to run, or to capture more profits when available.

Follow T.P: Did you follow your trading plan during this trade? - Or did you go rogue and just do it all yourself? Maybe you started using your trading plan for your entry but forgot about it during the trade and exited randomly? Only you truly know how accurately you followed along with *your* trading plan. A simple Yes/No answer is needed, and if you want to answer with; "Well, kind of," or "I half followed it," just go ahead and put No. 'Kind of' strategies aren't profitable over the long term, and neither will following the rules with a 'kind of' attitude.

Happy?: What are your initial thoughts concerning this trade? - This is fairly straightforward. Don't overthink it. Were you happy or not? Keep in mind, you can be happy with a trade that didn't go your way if you remain disciplined. You can also be unhappy with profitable trades if you broke your rules and got on the lucky side of a fundamental news push. Honesty is your best policy here.

Box 4:

In the first box on page 2 you will be explaining; why we are, or are not, happy with our trade. When you are beginning, you will most likely feel some sort of elation or disappointment with every trade you enter. This is normal. In fact, as you progress, this doesn't disappear completely, it just becomes better managed. After all, emotions are what make us human. I would be lying if I said I never felt emotions on the chart. The key is to understand why we are feeling those emotions and move on quickly without letting it affect us. In this box, I would like you to write down everything that is making you happy or unhappy regarding the trade. If you have mixed emotions, great, write it down. If you have no emotion, even better. Write this down also.

Box 5:

This box represents the emotions during Phase 3. It is important to write down all the emotions we are feeling now that the trade has been closed. You previously wrote down why you were or weren't happy with the trade. However, now that the trade is closed and you have had some time, what emotions are you feeling? Frustration in making the same mistakes? Disappointment in breaking your rules? Perhaps you are extremely proud because you followed all the rules and made some good profit. Whatever it is, write it down.

Box 6:
In our very last box, it is important to self-evaluate. What could you have done better during this particular trade? Perhaps you closed the trade unnecessarily? Maybe you were overpowered with emotion, or perhaps you could have trailed your stop loss tighter. Any improvements you believed would have helped you with this trade should be written down. We will use this information to help us select one of the 'Performance Review Keywords.' If you feel you made the perfect trade, then feel free to write nothing here. You will know deep down when you have done this and it will feel great. Later, in the following chapter, I will explain how you can set up your environment to hopefully increase the frequency of these trades. The 'Perfect' trades.

Performance Review Keywords:
Finally we have our very last box on the far right-hand side. It is much smaller than the rest because we will use it to summarize and categorize our key areas of improvement for each trade with one keyword. Below I have provided you with a list of the nine most common reasons, I believe, we make mistakes as new traders. All of these keywords/reasons are based on some level of emotion, either one of the four main fears of trading or some other aspect that we, as humans, allow ourselves to be manipulated by. I truly believe that no matter what you have put in box 6, it will relate to one of these keywords. Over time, we will be able to go back and use these keywords to understand the emotions that are controlling us as an individual, and thus use this information to understand the areas we need to improve. Refer to 'Keywords' below.

Remember earlier we discussed how fear and greed ran the global financial markets? Well, when we break it down a little further, we find that the four main fears of trading tend to stand out above the rest. These are; FOMO (the Fear Of Missing Out), the fear of being wrong, the fear of leaving money on the table, and the fear of letting profits turn into a loss. At some level, all of these fears can simultaneously be viewed from the perspective of greed. Whether you realize it or not, it is most likely some degree of these major emotions holding you back from the level of success you desire. Your greed, I say again, will be one of your biggest battles throughout your trading journey. Whether it is conscious or subconscious, you will *not* become a profitable trader until you have found a way to dive deep and remove greed from your belief system. It could be that you come from a poor family with a poverty mindset, or that you grew up being taught how precious or evil money is. Maybe you come from a rich family and are used to getting the things you want easily. Perhaps it is linked to getting that dopamine release when the idea of making easy money comes to the conscious mind. Whatever it is, driving this emotion, you will need to understand it at a much deeper level to overcome it and rebuild your relationship with money.

On Chart Emotions

As well as fear and greed, you may notice a few other emotions that present themselves whilst you are trading. These emotions may be easier to notice and therefore easier to track, although I believe these are all, at some level, a derivative of fear or greed. These other emotions include, but are not limited to;

Boredom: Sometimes we spend an hour or more on the charts, and nothing presents itself. This creates a feeling of boredom and we start to force trades, or 'find' trades when there aren't any that match our trading plan.

Excitement or Euphoria: Excitement and euphoria become present when you get a few really good trades and begin to feel like you are the king (or queen) of the charts and that every trade you take, will make you massive profits.

Agitation or frustration: This is when you feel every trade you make is a losing one and you're never going to be able to understand this skill which can sometimes lead to the notorious 'Fuck it Friday.' Don't worry, everyone feels this at some point or another. Just understand these are emotions speaking and not a true reflection of your trading ability.

Hope: Hope trading is when you begin to ignore your exits in the 'hope' your trade will turn around. This is common among those with bigger egos. Denying that they have made the wrong decision and refusing to close a trade early to protect capital.

Anxiety: If you ever felt anxious when in a trade, or stressed at the sight of how much drawdown you are in, then you are probably risking too much. Perhaps you're using too big of a lot size, you're overleveraged, or taking on too many positions at once.

Keywords

Now that we understand some of the major emotions you may experience during your trading journey, it is time to connect them to some of the more common trading errors that people make. By connecting these common trading mistakes with a simple keyword and the emotions or reasons for making these mistakes, I am hoping you can quickly establish and understand the areas that you, as an individual trader, need to improve on.

- **Forced Entry (FE):** This relates to when we begin feeling boredom. After spending large amounts of time on the charts with no good trades presenting themselves, we begin to force trades. This is usually due to a very common upbringing that teaches us to trade time for money. This is a derivative of greed, as we feel that after spending time watching the charts, we are owed a certain level of remuneration. If this occurs frequently, it is important to remind yourself of the power of compound interest, and remember, that it is imperative to put 'free' time into learning a skill that will eventually pay you for a lifetime. Time on live charts does *not* have to be paid time.

- **No Entry Entry (NEE):** This happens when you start to take entries that do not comply with your trading plan. If your plan says to wait for a particular fib level and you enter before it reaches it, that's a NEE. If you are meant to enter off a particular candle pattern, but it doesn't play out, and you still enter, that's a NEE. If you are just hitting the button because of a "*feeling*," that's a NEE. These are all No Entry Entries, and this comes from the fear of missing out. This also relates to greed, as you are essentially entering early in the fear the move will happen without you and you will miss the 'BIG MOVE'. Over time you will notice that these losses add up and outweigh those moves you *do* catch by entering early or randomly.

- **Revenge Entry (RE):** This entry is made straight after a loss or an early exit. This entry will sometimes meet your criteria, and sometimes it won't, but it is always fueled by emotion. For example, when you are frustrated at a loss and want to get your money back - Greed. A revenge entry may also come after getting taken out early and not wanting to miss the 'Big Move,' - FOMO/Greed. Revenge entries can happen quickly. This can compound and turn a bad day into a *very* bad day, or even a blown account. Often these will be

37

associated with over-trading and will be found towards the end of a trading day/session. It is *very* important to observe these, especially as a scalper. These should be the first keywords we aim to remove from our emotional journal as they can be like a virus. Once you have one, it's easy for more to follow.

- **Early Move to Break Even (E2BE):** As you get further down your trading journey, you understand how important it is to protect your capital. One common way of doing this is moving your 'Stop Loss' to 'Break Even' once the trade is in profit, for a 'Risk-Free' trade. However, if a trader feels anxious about the amount they are risking or fearful of losing money, they may move their stop loss too soon. Often price likes to retest levels before making its move, and moving your Stop Loss too early can result in the price returning, taking you out, and then making a large move in your predicted direction. This can be extremely frustrating when you are learning *and* when you're experienced. If this keyword repeats itself, you should look at reducing your risk per trade. This can be hard if you are a greedy trader, but you will make more profits in the long term, as you will be more open to giving the trade the room it needs to play out.

- **Ignoring Exits (Hope):** Ignoring all exits as your trade goes in the wrong direction is often referred to as hope trading. You have now detached yourself from your trading plan and are ignoring your rules in the hope your trade will turn around. More often than not, you will have legitimate excuses and justification for *why* you allow this to happen, but once you become honest with yourself and dig deeper you will learn it is your ego. This mistake usually relates to the fear of being wrong or the fear of losing money. Having an ego on the charts will destroy you. If you find this keyword repeating itself, don't be upset, even the most modest people will find they have an ego hiding within them once they begin the self-development program known as trading.

- **Random Exits (RandoE):** You may notice yourself randomly exiting trades without explanation. If this happens, it is important to understand the situation. Was the trade in profit? Were you fearful of letting profits turn into losses? Was the trade going in the wrong direction, leaving you unable to handle the stress of drawdown? Are you waiting for candle closure to make your decisions, or do you let the emotions of price action manipulate your actions? Once we begin doing things without explanation, we have strayed from our trading plan. It is important to be aware of these times and figure out more about the fear that caused it, aim to remove it and get back to using our trading plan.

- **Trailed too Aggressive (AT):** Finding the balance between taking profits and giving our trades room to run can be one of the hardest balancing acts. Whether you trail your stop loss or take partial profits, you may find yourself continuously doing this too soon or too aggressively. This often results in you exiting a trade that goes much further into profit, leaving you frustrated or disappointed. Often trailing too aggressively comes from having a fear of letting profits turn to losses, which can be associated with a poverty mindset when we are taught, from a young age, to protect our money at all costs. If this happens repeatedly, it is worth diving deeper into your relationship with money.

- **Trailed too Loosely (LT):** Much like the previous keyword, it's tough to find that balance between allowing your trade room to run and protecting your capital. If you find that you often leave a lot of profit on the table, only to have price pull *all the way* back and take you out of your trade, then perhaps you also need to look at your relationship with money. Trailing too loosely can come from a greed standpoint, or a fear of leaving points on the table. Again and again, we allow our trades extra room because we feel they could go on forever, making us rich with one huge trade. This is often not the case. You need to have modesty and gratitude when trading. If you continue to feel frustration that the price pulls back to take you out and that you gave up too many points, consider finding gratitude for the smaller amount of points you *do* have, and not be disappointed in the number of points you feel you *should* have had. This one can be as simple as changing your perspective. Rather than finding frustration in that which we feel we were owed, try practicing gratitude with the simple phrase "thank you stop loss." "Thank you for collecting my profits," or "thank you for protecting my capital." This simple verbalisation can be powerful to the subconscious mind.

- **Exaggerated Expectations (the Dreamer):** This last keyword also expands from the previous one. When we enter a trade, it is

39

important to know where the trade is expected to go. This could be; a previous structure, an EMA, a fib level, or any other area relative to your style. Some people set take profits which is an easy way to take the points you are aiming for. Others will trail stop losses or take manual exits. The key is not to change your expectations during a trade. Often as a trade moves to a particular level, we can get greedy and say. "Well, if it breaks this level, it will go up to here." This is what I call exaggerated expectations, or moving the goalposts. When the price reaches your expected level, remember your gratitude and modesty and be sure to secure a large portion, if not all, of your profit. If you find yourself giving it room to break the levels, and are disappointed when it rejects that level and pulls back a long way to take you out, then you should re-establish your relationship with money and greed.

As you can see, all of the more common mistakes (above) made by developing traders, can be related to emotion. Most of these can be brought back to one form of fear or greed, usually due to our upbringing and relationship with money. This makes sense as we have all come from different backgrounds and are taught different beliefs and values. The key aspect here is to quickly learn on a deeper level, who we are as both; a trader, and a human. By noticing and tracking our repeated behaviors, we can dive deeper and redirect our beliefs and values to avoid the pitfalls that hold us back from the next level of success. Now you might find that there are other common mistakes you are making, which is perfectly normal. If you find there is something not on the list, then feel free to add it. On the same level, you can rephrase the keywords to any verbiage you so desire. The important thing is that you have an easy, trackable, and relatable list of common mistakes and the reason and emotions behind these mistakes. Most traders are more than happy to hold onto their losing trades, but will struggle to let their winning trades run. We want to track our emotions to enhance our ability to allow the opposite to occur.

Now that we have the perfect recipe for developing ourselves as a trader, wouldn't it be nice if we had a way to speed up the learning process? Well, with a few clever little psychological tricks and hacks, we can enhance our learning with little to no added effort. Without going into too much depth, the last chapter in this incredible journal guide 'Environment is Everything' will be aimed at how we can trick our brains and optimize our learning.

Environment is Everything

(How to Optimize your Learning)

"Tell me and I forget, teach me and I may remember, involve me and I learn."

- Benjamin Franklin

Learning to trade can be one hell of a journey. Something that will take time, dedication, heartache, loss, and plenty of frustration. However, the reason I refer to it as; "the best personal development program in the world," is that to be successful at it, you need to be willing to dig deep and actually make the required changes. You need to have the willingness to learn about yourself on a very deep level, and the persistence to continue growing even through all the failures and struggles. Over a long period of time, what this does to a person is incredible. The resilience, discipline, and emotional intelligence you can build along the way is unimaginable. However, these character changes are not easy. The ones who will prevail in the long run are those few people willing to learn to look deep inside themselves, continue through the struggles, and do the required work.

How Long?

A very common question I get asked is, How long will this take me? And I ALWAYS respond with; It's not about how much time you spend on the charts, but how quickly you are willing to peel back your own layers and learn about yourself. You see, some of us have mountains of shit we need to dig through, while others have very little. It's the speed at which you are willing to progress yourself that determines the amount of time you need to become successful in this art. But there are ways to speed this process up. You see there are two types of people in this world; The ones who will read through this guide from front to back with the intention to make huge changes, only to put it in the closet, and use it as a dust collector; and those who will go through each step presented, fill out the information when asked, and consistently track their emotions and trades until they become successful traders. I have created this chapter to help those of you in the second category to optimize your learning and get the most out of this journal.

Hack the Brain

There are many little brain hacks that we can use to help accelerate our learning process with little to no extra effort. In fact, many of these aspects are built into the design of this journal. For example, the ability to only fill in five trades per day is subconsciously training you to reduce your number of trades, without you even thinking about it. For many, the need to turn to a new page and use a fresh sheet of paper is more effort than getting off the charts. Maybe you noticed that I have designed the cover of this journal with a sense of elegance. You are soon to be a professional trader. You should hold pride in this. By visually seeing and touching your gold-lettered journal, you can feel a sense of pride in what you are about to achieve. Now, this is available as an e-book, but I would highly suggest getting the hard copy and putting it on your desk in front of your computer. This very act will substantially increase the likelihood of you *actually* using it. As it now sits in your trading space, as a visual reminder for you to use it. Not on a file in the back of your computer. You can now see, smell, touch, and even taste it if you so choose. (I wouldn't recommend it, although I know a couple of you are thinking about it!) Furthermore, the order this journal has been laid out, will help you go through the necessary routine required to be consistent and profitable in the markets. Reinforcing your why and biggest dreams/desires daily. Going over your trade objectives and understanding the type of trader you are and the rules you have made for yourself, as well as reading any and *all* affirmations you have written aimed at getting you in a positive state of mind for trading. **Every Single Day.** You see, the environment is everything, we need to start setting up our external environment for peak efficiency so that we can spend more of our energy developing our internal environment. You now know how important tracking your emotions are, as well as going through and analyzing them, but will you do it?

Other tricks we can use are: Get yourself a nice pen that you use specifically for your trading journal. Just holding this pen will bring the association to the good behaviors of tracking your emotions, "that's my journaling pen", you will say to others, with a sense of pride, due to the fact you are successfully journaling your trading emotions. It comes with the undertone that you are serious about this. Furthermore, you can use different colored highlighters associated with each keyword that you use, for faster and better memory of the keyword and the recognition of repetition. At a glance, if your page is all green you know there is something that stands out for you to work on. I would also associate the colors green with greed and maybe red with fear. Be creative. This will make your analytical sessions at the end of each month, visually appealing and very easy to understand. A simple gold star is a subconscious reinforcement of good behavior. You should take note every time you follow your trading plan perfectly, whether it is profitable or not. If you make a 'perfect trade' and have nothing to write in the 'what you could have improved' box, then give yourself a gold star. You can then work towards filling your book with gold stars. A book full of gold stars is hard *not* to be proud of and smile at, as silly as it may feel to you. Lastly, be sure to make this book your own, add your flavor, and write your name in it. Personalize it. I can assure you this is going to add a whole new dimension to your trading. Also, be sure to create your 'Trading Plan' properly and also print it out, placing it right on the desk, next to this journal. I repeat, having these things that you can see, smell, touch, and hear will increase the chances of you using them regularly. We have multiple senses for a reason, use them. AND DO THE THINGS THAT ARE SUGGESTED! You can not expect to get the results associated with great success without doing the work that successful people are doing. Remember, 'environment is everything'. Set yourself up for success, not for failure. Life is hard enough. Spend a few minutes making it easy for yourself.

Monthly Analysis

(The 'Next-Level' trade analysis)

"Success comes to those who do not waste time looking and criticizing what others are doing, but focusing on honest self-evaluation and what they have to do."

– Amit Abraham

Up until now, you have been learning how to successfully and consistently track and analyze each of your trades, but now it's time to analyze your analysis. In the back of this journal, I have provided room to analyze and record your progress from month to month. You can do this at the end of each month or the beginning of the next. Whichever you choose, you must spend some quality time going through your journal and evaluating your progress. This is a **key** component of tracking and journaling. Just like you may do performance reviews at your job, you should be doing a review of your trading performance, but instead of 'review,' let's call it your 'monthly motivator.' It sounds a little more inviting. This is a time when you 'get' to go back and look at the progress you have made on your journey thus far. Remember, this is a long-term progressive skill that needs continuous development. It is *not* just a couple of months, a 'make or break' type of thing like many think. Each month you need to go through all your trades and fill in the information in the back. You will learn what works well for you, what doesn't, what emotions you have while trading, and what things you can improve on. You will notice whether or not you are sticking to your trading plan and if you aren't. Each month you will have an opportunity to refine your trading, and I suggest re-adjusting your trading plan every six months if you so desire. Just like spending twenty minutes at the end of each session is extremely important, so is spending a few hours at the end of each month finding progressive motivation, you can use, for bettering your skills. Furthermore, if you fill this out as intended, you will have all your trading information in one place, which is very helpful for your tax at the end of the year. Your accountant will thank you.

Please understand the importance of adequate testing time needed before changing any strategy. Especially when you start, I wouldn't change your trading plan until at least three months of tracking, at minimum, has been done. This ensures that the strategy has been used on a substantial number of trades and that you have adequate results to compare to. If you do wish to test a new strategy, this journal will be your best friend, however, I would highly recommend using a separate journal for each strategy. If you want to trade multiple strategies, then separate journals and trading accounts should be used for each. This allows for proper analysis of each strategy and ensures that your account balance is a true representation of the strategy, without your balance or emotions being affected by other strategies. For example, swing trading crypto and scalping commodities, forex trading and trading indices, or even two different strategies on the same pair. Whatever it may be, separate journals and accounts are recommended.

Get in Contact

If you have enjoyed the information in this guide, I would highly recommend getting yourself the bigger, blank emotional journal. This journal will allow you to continue recording and tracking your emotions all through your trading journey. Having your why, dreams, affirmations, trading objectives, and trading rules all in one convenient location, will help to keep a level of consistency in your trading routines, and give you the drive to keep going when times get tough. This consistency over time, crossed with a driven desire to succeed, is what will get you the results you are chasing.

I have provided a fair bit of information in this journal on the basis that you already have a certain level of trading knowledge. However, if you are just beginning or struggling in any particular area, do not hesitate to get in touch. I am always open to helping new and aspiring traders. Perhaps you haven't narrowed down your strategy, maybe you are wanting a change in learning, or perhaps you want further mindset training, it does not matter, I would love to help. I have a live mindset call, three times a week that you are welcome to join as well as plenty of direction to training materials, live trading sessions, and one on one coaching for special circumstances. I have a podcast that is aimed at developing the mindset and behaviors in both the trading environment and in most other areas of life and have created an ebook, a trading plan course and a mindset course that is soon to be released. To be put on the wait list for this course, or to get a copy of my new ebook, please scan the QR code or visit thttps://thepipside.mykajabi.com

If any of this further information is of interest to you, don't hesitate to reach out or simply scan the QR code on the next page. My podcast is called 'The Success Shift with Jake Snedker' and can be found on many of the main streaming platforms. You can also reach me on Facebook @Jakobe Shnediko, on Instagram @thesuccesfulhippie, or via email, at jakesnedker@gmail.com or thesuccessfulhippie@gmail.com all of which can be found by scanning the QR code.

I desire to give you the guidance, knowledge, and materials for you to help yourself in whatever direction you so choose to head. I thank you for your support and look forward to being in contact with you. If we do not cross paths again, I wish you all the best on your journey, wherever it may take you.

Scan Me! It's Fun

Before you dive into the incredible journaling section that follows, I want to ask you for just one *small* favor. If you have been able to take even one thing away from this journal that you feel will help you on *your* trading journey, then it would mean the world to me if you spend two minutes leaving me a short review on whichever platform you bought this book. This helps promote my book to other struggling traders that could benefit from this journal and allows me to continue creating quality learning material. Thank you in advance and happy trading.

Day:

Date:	W/L
Time:	T.T
Pair	WT/CT
B/S	P/L

1) Reason for entering the trade?

2) How did you feel before the trade?

3) How did/do you feel during the trade?

Date:	W/L
Time:	T.T
Pair	WT/CT
B/S	P/L

1) Reason for entering the trade?

2) How did you feel before the trade?

3) How did/do you feel during the trade?

Date:	W/L
Time:	T.T
Pair	WT/CT
B/S	P/L

1) Reason for entering the trade?

2) How did you feel before the trade?

3) How did/do you feel during the trade?

Date:	W/L
Time:	T.T
Pair	WT/CT
B/S	P/L

1) Reason for entering the trade?

2) How did you feel before the trade?

3) How did/do you feel during the trade?

Date:	W/L
Time:	T.T
Pair	WT/CT
B/S	P/L

1) Reason for entering the trade?

2) How did you feel before the trade?

3) How did/do you feel during the trade?

My Emotional Trading Journal

Exit Strat	4) Why were you Happy/ Unhappy with this Trade?	5) How did you feel after the trade?	6) What could you have improved on?	Keyword
Actual Exit				
Follow T.P?				
Happy?				

Exit Strat	4) Why were you Happy/ Unhappy with this Trade?	5) How did you feel after the trade?	6) What could you have improved on?	Keyword
Actual Exit				
Follow T.P?				
Happy?				

Exit Strat	4) Why were you Happy/ Unhappy with this Trade?	5) How did you feel after the trade?	6) What could you have improved on?	Keyword
Actual Exit				
Follow T.P?				
Happy?				

Exit Strat	4) Why were you Happy/ Unhappy with this Trade?	5) How did you feel after the trade?	6) What could you have improved on?	Keyword
Actual Exit				
Follow T.P?				
Happy?				

Exit Strat	4) Why were you Happy/ Unhappy with this Trade?	5) How did you feel after the trade?	6) What could you have improved on?	Keyword
Actual Exit				
Follow T.P?				
Happy?				

Day:

Date:	W/L
Time:	T.T
Pair	WT/CT
B/S	P/L

1) Reason for entering the trade?

2) How did you feel before the trade?

3) How did/do you feel during the trade?

Date:	W/L
Time:	T.T
Pair	WT/CT
B/S	P/L

1) Reason for entering the trade?

2) How did you feel before the trade?

3) How did/do you feel during the trade?

Date:	W/L
Time:	T.T
Pair	WT/CT
B/S	P/L

1) Reason for entering the trade?

2) How did you feel before the trade?

3) How did/do you feel during the trade?

Date:	W/L
Time:	T.T
Pair	WT/CT
B/S	P/L

1) Reason for entering the trade?

2) How did you feel before the trade?

3) How did/do you feel during the trade?

Date:	W/L
Time:	T.T
Pair	WT/CT
B/S	P/L

1) Reason for entering the trade?

2) How did you feel before the trade?

3) How did/do you feel during the trade?

My Emotional Trading Journal

Exit Strat	
Actual Exit	
Follow T.P?	
Happy?	

4) Why were you Happy/Unhappy with this Trade?

5) How did you feel after the trade?

6) What could you have improved on?

Keyword

Exit Strat	
Actual Exit	
Follow T.P?	
Happy?	

4) Why were you Happy/Unhappy with this Trade?

5) How did you feel after the trade?

6) What could you have improved on?

Keyword

Exit Strat	
Actual Exit	
Follow T.P?	
Happy?	

4) Why were you Happy/Unhappy with this Trade?

5) How did you feel after the trade?

6) What could you have improved on?

Keyword

Exit Strat	
Actual Exit	
Follow T.P?	
Happy?	

4) Why were you Happy/Unhappy with this Trade?

5) How did you feel after the trade?

6) What could you have improved on?

Keyword

Exit Strat	
Actual Exit	
Follow T.P?	
Happy?	

4) Why were you Happy/Unhappy with this Trade?

5) How did you feel after the trade?

6) What could you have improved on?

Keyword

Trading Plan Example

ARE YOU IN A HAPPY AND/OR NEUTRAL FRAME OF MIND??

YOU DON'T HAVE TO TRADE EVERY DAY

REMEMBER; "NO TRADE, IS STILL A GOOD TRADE"

Pre-trading Check-list

- What way is the market trending overall?

- What way is the market trending on 15 min and lower time frames?

- Are there any major Support and Resistance (Daily)?

- What Lot size are you using/ What size SL = 1% or 2%?

DON'T RUSH INTO ANY TRADES

CHECK YOUR GREED

YOU ONLY NEED 1% PER SESSION TO HAVE A VERY GOOD WEEK

ENJOY IT. BE PRESENT IN EVERY MOMENT
LIFE IS MEANT TO BE LIVED AND EXPERIENCED

YOUR IDEAL TRADE IS A BUY 'DELO' WITH THE AQUA CUTTING
THROUGH

Entry Check-list

Price Action CL

- ☐ Bullish/Bearish (other boss candles) Engulfing candle? (1 point)

- ☐ Is the Aqua cutting through? (1 point)

- ☐ Is it with the Trend? (1 point)

- ☐ Is it on the second leg of a W/M? (1 point)

- ☐ After the Red and Yellow cross? (1 point)
  - ☐ Less than 5 candles after the cross? (Bonus: 1 point)

TDI CL

Where is price?

- ☐ Outside the Volatility Band on the opposite side to trend? (5 points)

- ☐ In the Entry Zone, and crossed the Liquid 50 (L50)? (4 points)

- ☐ In the Entry Zone but heading into the L50? (3 points)
  - possibly wait for LC Cross Entry

- ☐ Just above the 60/ Just below the 40 - in the direction of the trade ? (2 points)

- ☐ Heading into the 60 or above the 70/ heading into the 40 or below the 30? (1 point)

- ☐ Outside the VB in the direction of the trade? (0 points)

What is your trade score? | If 7+ then you enter the trade

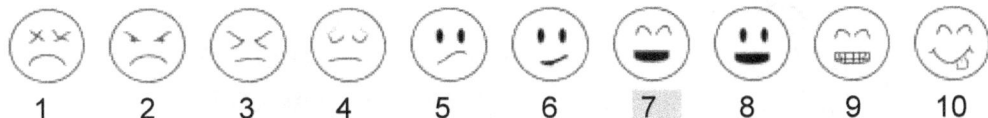

1	2	3	4	5	6	7	8	9	10

WAIT FOR A PULLBACK TO THE YELLOW
THERE WILL ALWAYS BE MORE TRADES
YOU ARE PAID FOR YOUR PATIENCE

Know your position

You have found a good trade setup. GREAT. Now you need to know.....

- Is your SL greater than 1.5x your calculated points?
  If so you need to change your lot size

- Do you know your estimated Take Profit?
  Previous Structure, EMA. What are you targeting?

- What is your desired R:R roughly?

- How volatile is the current market? What is the average candle size/volume?

- You need to look for an Exit that is roughly half the size of your estimated TP - PROTECT YOUR CAPITAL!!

Maximum Loss Exit is your SL. This should ALWAYS BE PUT IN PLACE to stop you from emotionally getting dragged down with a trade (Spread x2 below lowest previous low)

EXITS CL (Pick at least ONE)

Reduced loss exits.

- ☐ Entry Zone Exit
- ☐ KC Exit
- ☐ LC Exit
- ☐ 3COL Exit (Delo)
- ☐ 8COL Exit

Profitable exits

- ☐ VBC Exit
- ☐ TSI Exit (Green and Red Cross)
- ☐ KC Exit
- ☐ Trailing SL (What is your happy profit amount?)
- ☐ Inside bar opposite candle Exit (Price Action Exit)

AS THE CHART MOVES SIDEWAYS THE ANALYSIS CHANGES

DON'T SIT IN A TRADE THAT IS GOING NOWHERE

STARTING ACC BAL		BUY	WINS	LESSONS
CLOSING ACC BAL		SELL		
TOTAL NO. TRADES		W/L		
PROFIT		L/S		

HOW DO YOU FEEL YOU TRADED THIS MONTH?

ARE YOU HAPPY/PROUD OF YOUR PROGRESS THIS PAST MONTH? HOW WELL DID YOU STICK TO YOUR TRADING PLAN?

STARTING ACC BAL		BUY	WINS	LESSONS
CLOSING ACC BAL		SELL		
TOTAL NO. TRADES		W/L		
PROFIT		L/S		

HOW DO YOU FEEL YOU TRADED THIS MONTH?

ARE YOU HAPPY/PROUD OF YOUR PROGRESS THIS PAST MONTH? HOW WELL DID YOU STICK TO YOUR TRADING PLAN?

STARTING ACC BAL		BUY	WINS	LESSONS
CLOSING ACC BAL		SELL		
TOTAL NO. TRADES		W/L		
PROFIT		L/S		

HOW DO YOU FEEL YOU TRADED THIS MONTH?

ARE YOU HAPPY/PROUD OF YOUR PROGRESS THIS PAST MONTH? HOW WELL DID YOU STICK TO YOUR TRADING PLAN?

Notes from this quater:

TOP KEYWORD THIS MONTH

EMOTION ASSOCIATED W KEYWORD

SECOND TOP KEYWORD

EMOTION ASSOCIATED W KEYWORD

TOP KEYWORD THIS MONTH

EMOTION ASSOCIATED W KEYWORD

SECOND TOP KEYWORD

EMOTION ASSOCIATED W KEYWORD

TOP KEYWORD THIS MONTH

EMOTION ASSOCIATED W KEYWORD

SECOND TOP KEYWORD

EMOTION ASSOCIATED W KEYWORD

Notes from this quater:

www.ingramcontent.com/pod-product-compliance
Lightning Source LLC
Chambersburg PA
CBHW030534210326
41597CB00014B/1145